86 Ways to Cope When the Red Sox DON'T Win

by Melinda R. Boroson

with illustrations by Nathan Y. Jarvis

Brown House BOOKS

Text and illustrations © 2008 Brown House Books

For information about permission to reproduce selections from this book, write to: Permissions, Brown House Books, 95 Sawyer Road, Suite 400, Waltham, MA 02453. www.brownhousebooks.com

ISBN: 978-0-9767938-2-3

Printed in the United States of America
1 2 3 4 5 6 7 8 9 10 DSG 12 11 10 9 8

Also from Brown House Books
86 Years: The Legend of the Boston Red Sox

Dedicated to the fans of Red Sox Nation
who *always* remain faithful and hopeful—
even when the Sox don't win.

Acknowledgments

Many thanks to Kim Gonzaga, Aimee Meacham,
and Hannah Ruderman, Red Sox fans extraordinaire,
for their contributions to *86 Ways*.

Special thanks to Kathy Reynolds, Monica Ann Crigler,
and Joe Hinckley for defying gravity and surpassing
the speed of light to produce this book.

Introduction

Nobody dreams or despairs like Red Sox fans. Their hearts soar, leap, swell, stop, ache, break, mend, and live to beat again—sometimes all in the course of a single inning.

When the Red Sox win—well, that's pure joy, and we don't think you need any help figuring out how to celebrate.

But, when the Red Sox lose. Ah, that's another story. Gloom and doom envelop you. A dark cloud follows you as you try to go about your daily routine. It hurts. It really does.

How do you snap out of it? How do you cope? Maybe by remembering past Red Sox glory. Maybe by considering the wisdom of the world's greatest philosophers. Maybe by grabbing another beer and weeping openly.

Here are 86 ways.

Go Sox!

Marie Brown
Melinda Boroson
Brown House Books

"Only those who have endured the greatest suffering can become the greatest people."

— Chinese proverb

Don't let anybody tell you that Red Sox fans are not the greatest people!

..PLEASE, *Please*, PLEASE, PUH-LEEZE!

Pray that the Red Sox start winning again.
You never know, it might work!

3

"One does not love
a place the less for
having suffered in it
unless it has
all been suffering,
nothing but suffering."

— Jane Austen (1775–1817)
English novelist

Obviously, Jane Austen was
talking about Fenway.

Go to sleep in your rally cap
and let it do its work overnight.

5

"Out of suffering have emerged the strongest souls; the most massive characters are seared with scars."

— Kahlil Gibran (1883–1931)
Lebanese/American poet and essayist

Yes, that Red Sox tattoo you got in 1986 counts as a scar.

Start running and don't stop
until you are ready to drop.
Exhaustion will help you forget.

7

"We are healed
of a suffering
only by expressing
it to the full."

— Marcel Proust (1871–1922)
French novelist

In other words—go ahead, weep!

8

Carl Yastrzemski

Led the American League
in batting average, home runs,
and RBIs in 1967.

9

Ted Williams

The greatest hitter in baseball history.

10

Curse! Shout every swear word you know
at the top of your lungs.
(If you live in an apartment, better do this in
the bathroom with the shower running.)

11

"If we will be quiet and ready enough, we shall find compensation in every disappointment."

— Henry David Thoreau (1817–1862)
U.S. philosopher

Might Thoreau have been
a Red Sox fan?

12

1912—The Red Sox win the World Series and Fenway Park opens.

13

Recognize that you are a victim of
Repetitive **E**nthusiasm **D**isorder
with **S**port **O**bsession e**X**haustion.
Seek professional help.

14

"Every great mistake
has a halfway moment,
a split second when
it can be recalled
and perhaps remedied."

— Pearl S. Buck (1982–1973)
American writer and Nobel Prize winner

Or watched again and again on
instant replay to REALLY rub it in.

15

Take heart: If you got over Bill B**kner,
you can survive anything.

16

Gather family and friends together
for group hugs, commiseration, and beer.

"Patience and perseverance have a magical effect before which difficulties disappear and obstacles vanish."

— John Quincy Adams (1767–1848)
U.S. president

With that attitude, he COULDN'T have been a Red Sox fan.

18

Johnny Damon

Come on! When he was ours,
he was a hero.

19

"There are occasions when it is undoubtedly better to incur loss than to make gain."

— Plautus (254–184 BC)
ancient Greek playwright

But those occasions don't happen during April, May, June, July, August, September, or October.

20

Try to believe the old saw:
"After all, it's only a game."

21

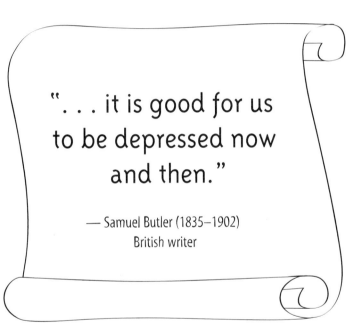

"... it is good for us to be depressed now and then."

— Samuel Butler (1835–1902)
British writer

Well, as long as it's GOOD for us ...

22

Remember that baseball is a "streaky" game—
a string of losses will soon enough
become a string of wins.

"The best thing about
the future is that
it only comes one day
at a time."

— Abraham Lincoln (1809–1865)
U.S. president

Except for double-headers.

24

Invite friends over to watch your DVD of
Games 4, 5, 6, and 7 of the 2004 ALCS.
Pretend they are happening live.

25

"We need as much something to suffer for as something to live for."

— Eric Hoffer (1902–1983)
U.S. philosopher

Red Sox Nation has had
a lifetime supply of both.

26

Remember that The Jimmy Fund
is a beautiful thing.
Make a donation.

27

Carlton Fisk

Waving that home run into fair territory—
beautiful!

28

Take a shower right away. Put on your PJs
and think about how we are
due for a win tomorrow.

29

"Difficulties increase the nearer we get to the goal."

— Goethe (1749–1832)
German writer

That must explain October.

Call a buddy and have a serious discussion about how George Steinbrenner has ruined Major League Baseball. Feel good knowing that your team is honest and fair.

Embrace the loss.
Underdog is what we do best.

32

"Everything hurts."

— Michelangelo (1474–1564)
Italian Renaissance painter and sculptor

You should try painting a ceiling while
listening to the Red Sox lose a game.
THEN tell me about pain.

33

Invite friends to a barbecue and reminisce about the great Red Sox games you've seen.

34

Big Papi's walk-off homer in
do-or-die Game 4 of the ALCS 2004

"If you're going through hell, keep going."

— Winston Churchill (1874–1965)
British prime minister

England made it through
the Blitz—you can get over
a mid-season slump.

36

Watch the news.
You'll find something more important
to be upset about.

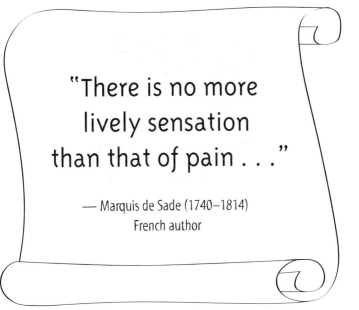

"There is no more
lively sensation
than that of pain . . ."

— Marquis de Sade (1740–1814)
French author

Why are we not surprised that
the namesake of sadism
had something to say about the Red Sox?

38

Curt Schilling and the bloody sock:
The definition of fortitude.

39

Tuck your kids in with a bedtime story
about how heroes never give up.

Reconsider that offer from the devil.

41

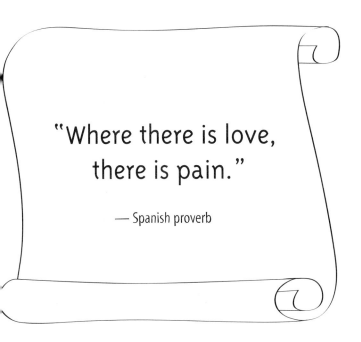

"Where there is love,
there is pain."

— Spanish proverb

If you don't know that already,
you can't call yourself a Red Sox fan.

Immediately tune in to the Yankee game
and root for the opposing team.

43

"A man who suffers before it is necessary, suffers more than is necessary."

— Seneca (4 BC–65 AD)
ancient Roman statesman and philosopher

So try to keep your blood pressure under control—at least through the national anthem.

44

Take up yoga.
It will fill you with a sense of peace and calm.

45

Take up juggling. It will fill you with a sense of anger and frustration.

(Either way, you'll get your mind off the game!)

46

Misery loves company: Remember that there are millions and millions of Red Sox fans all over the world.

47

"Show me a good loser
and I'll show you
an idiot."

— Leo Durocher (1905–1991)
American baseball player/manager

And your mama didn't raise an idiot—
am I right?

48

Don't be a fair-weather fan:
Write a letter to your favorite Red Sox player
and tell him why he's the greatest.

49

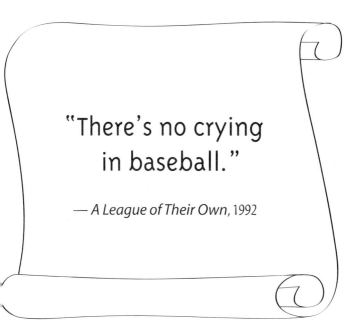

"There's no crying
in baseball."

— *A League of Their Own*, 1992

And yet, sometimes, there is.

Repeat three times:
The Curse is broken.
The Curse is broken.
The Curse is broken.

Think about why you truly love
the game of baseball.

52

"We are not interested in
the possibilities of defeat;
they do not exist."

— Queen Victoria (1819–1901)
ruler of Great Britain

And while we're at it,
the Yankees don't exist either!

Queen of Denial
1918–2004

53

ALCS 2004 vs. the Yankees—
The greatest comeback
in sports history.

54

Take the dog for a walk.
Discuss the team's woes.

55

Hug your cat.

56

Call your dad and reminisce about
the first game you watched together.

57

"Suffering becomes beautiful when anyone bears great calamities with cheerfulness."

— Aristotle (384–322 BC)
ancient Greek philosopher

And what's more beautiful
than a Red Sox fan?

58

Read "Casey at the Bat" aloud,
but substitute "Jeter" for Casey.
(He strikes out, you know.)

59

"Success is the ability to go from one failure to another with no loss of enthusiasm."

— Winston Churchill (1874–1965)
British prime minister

The very definition of a
"successful" Red Sox fan.

60

Eat a Fenway Frank.
Then go to bed.

61

Eat a carton of "Curse Reversed" ice cream.
Then go to bed.

62

"Many of life's failures
are people who did not
realize how close
they were to success
when they gave up."

— Thomas Alva Edison (1847–1931)
American inventor

But a true Red Sox fan
will NEVER leave a game before the end.
We never give up hope!

Reread
86 Years: The Legend of the Boston Red Sox.
You'll feel great!
Guaranteed.

64

Rant on your Red Sox blog.

65

On the slim chance that you don't already
have a Red Sox blog, start one.

"No matter how hard the loss, defeat might serve as well as victory to shake the soul and let the glory out."

— Al Gore (b. 1948)
U.S. vice-president, 2000 presidential candidate

And he oughta know.

67

1967: The Impossible Dream

68

"No one is more
miserable than the person
who wills everything
and can do nothing."

— Claudius (10 BC– 54 AD)
Roman emperor

If only YOU managed the team,
then we'd be winning, right?

Change your lucky socks.
Everyone will be better off.

"We have resolved to endure the unendurable and suffer what is insufferable."

— Hirohito (1901–1989) Japanese emperor

Who knew there were
Red Sox fans in Japan
before Daisuke joined the team?

71

Rookie Clay Buchholz's no-hitter,
September 1, 2007

Jon Lester's no-hitter,
May 19, 2008

"In three words I can
sum up everything I've
learned about life:
it goes on."

Robert Frost (1874–1963)
U.S. poet

Further proof that baseball = life.

Teach the dog a new trick.

74

"Adversity and loss
make a man wise."

— Welsh proverb

Don't you feel yourself getting
wiser by the minute?

75

Game 6 of the 1975 World Series—
The greatest World Series Game ever.

"We must accept
finite disappointment,
but never lose
infinite hope."

— Dr. Martin Luther King, Jr. (1929–1968)
U.S. civil rights leader

And that's what it takes to be
a member of Red Sox Nation.

77

Sing "Sweet Caroline"
at the top of your lungs:
"So good, so good, so good!"

78

October 16, 2008
ALCS Game 5

Facing elimination and down 7-0 in
the 7th inning, the Red Sox rally to beat
the Tampa Bay Rays 8-7—the greatest
comeback in post-season history since 1929!

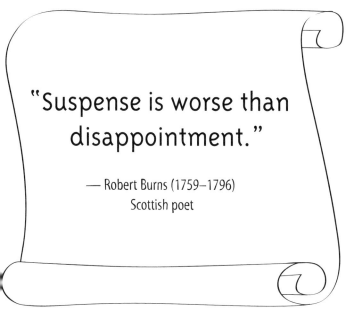

"Suspense is worse than disappointment."

— Robert Burns (1759–1796)
Scottish poet

But suspense followed by disappointment
really sucks.

Watch *Fever Pitch* until the
bad feelings go away.

81

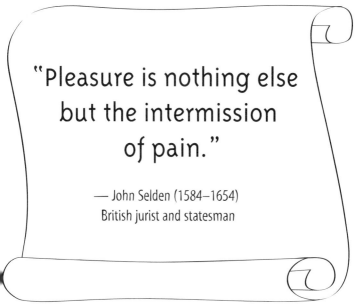

"Pleasure is nothing else
but the intermission
of pain."

— John Selden (1584–1654)
British jurist and statesman

Same goes for
the seventh-inning stretch.

82

October 27, 2004:
Does it get any better than that?

83

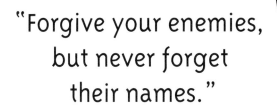

"Forgive your enemies,
but never forget
their names."

— John F. Kennedy (1917–1963)
U.S. president

Babe Ruth, Bucky "F." Dent,
Derek Jeter, A-Rod ...

84

World champions again!
October 28, 2007

85

"Don't look forward to the day you stop suffering, because when it comes you'll know you're dead."

— Tennessee Williams (1911–1983)
U.S. playwright

Amen.

86

Let's face it.
Nothing is going to make you feel better
until the Red Sox win again!

What's YOUR way to cope?